STEP-UP HISTORY

The Irish Diaspora

Sean Sheehan

Evans

Published by Evans Brothers Limited
2A Portman Mansions
Chiltern Street
London W1U 6NR

© Evans Brothers Limited 2008

Produced for Evans Brothers Limited by
White-Thomson Publishing Ltd,
Bridgewater Business Centre,
210 High Street,
Lewes, East Sussex BN7 2NH

Printed in Hong Kong by New Era Printing Co. Ltd.

Project manager: Sonya Newland

Designer: Robert Walster

Consultant: Brian Malone

British Library Cataloguing in Publication Data

Sheehan, Sean
The diaspora. - (Step up history)

1. Irish - Foreign countries - Juvenile literature
2. Ireland - Emigration and immigration -
History
Juvenile literature

I. Title
941'.0049162

ISBN-13: 9780237534318

Picture acknowledgements:

Alamy: pages 5 and cover top left (Bernie Epstein),
11 (Michael Diggin), 21 (Wim Wiskereke), 27 (Eric
James); Corbis: pages 1, 9 (Jeremy Horner), 13, 15
(Bettmann), 16, 17b and cover (Bettmann), 18, 22
(Hulton Deutsch Collection), 24 (Hulton Deutsch
Collection), 25 and cover top right (DW/For
Picture); iStock: pages 14 (Royce DeGrie), 17t, 20;
Mary Evans Picture Library: pages 8; Shutterstock:
page 26; Topfoto.co.uk: pages 7 (AA World Travel
Library), 12 (Topham Picturepoint), 23.

Illustrative work by Robert Walster.

Contents

What is the Diaspora?

Today, Ireland is home to people of many races, but for centuries very few people from other countries came to Ireland. In fact, native Irish men and women left their country to find new homes abroad. Between 1700 and today, about 10 million Irish people settled in other countries. These people and their descendants have become known as the Diaspora.

Reasons for the Diaspora

For lots of Irish people the word Diaspora is a sad one, because many of those who left Ireland did not want to go. They felt they had no choice. In the eighteenth century, Ireland was ruled by Britain and under British law, crimes like taking part in a rebellion or stealing even quite small things could be punished by transportation. Men, women and even children were sent away to Australia or America, where they were put in prison factories or made to work as slaves on farms.

It was not only criminals who were forced to leave Ireland, though. Ordinary people were desperately poor and often hungry. Many left Ireland voluntarily

1500s Irish people form part of the first white settlement in South America.

1652–57 50,000 Irish people are transported to the Caribbean.

1704 Irish people leave for America rather than join the Church of England.

1790 Transportation of criminals to the Caribbean ends.

50 **1600** 1650 **1700** 1750

1583 1,000 rebels leave Ireland to join the armies of Europe.

1691 The Treaty of Limerick – 16,000 Irish men are forced to join European armies.

1720–76 Transportation of about 200 criminals and rebels to America each year.

in the hope of finding a better life abroad. The Great Famine (1845–51) also forced people to leave. In more recent times, they left in search of better jobs and quality of life than they felt they could get in Ireland. Today, their children and grandchildren are proud to have Irish ancestors.

About this book

In this book you will find out about the different people who made up the Irish Diaspora and why they left their country. You will learn where they travelled to and what life was like for them when they got there.

One of the reasons for the Diaspora was the Great Famine. This Famine memorial is in Pennsylvania, USA, and shows Irish people arriving in the United States.

1791–1868 48,000 Irish people are transported to prison colonies in Australia.

1860–72 Irish soldiers in the British army fight Maori tribes in New Zealand.

1939 The Second World War begins – numbers of Irish immigrants to Britain increase.

1970–80 The Irish become the largest immigrant group in Britain.

800 **1850** **1900** **1950** **200**

1845–51 The Great Famine. Thousands leave for Britain, Canada and America.

1868 The last ship carrying criminals to Australia from Ireland brings 62 rebels.

1880 40,000 Irish people settled in Argentina.

2000s Immigration to Ireland exceeds emigration.

The Wild Geese

From the sixteenth century to the eighteenth century, thousands of Irish men left Ireland for Europe. They went to fight as mercenaries in the wars between the kings of Europe. Many of them had rebelled against the English, who ruled Ireland, and had to leave after their rebellions were defeated. They went to Spain, France or Holland. Smaller numbers joined the armies of Germany and Russia. They went to the countries that offered the most money for their fighting skills, and they formed special groups called Irish brigades.

▲ Irish brigades could be found in many parts of Europe by the end of the seventeenth century.

Rebels abroad

The English government encouraged rebels to join foreign armies. Sometimes the government even paid for their passage to Europe. Why do you think the government would do this? What problems might the rebels later cause? Make a list of the pros and cons of sending the rebels abroad to fight for other countries.

Pros	Cons

The first big emigration of Irish men came in 1583, after the defeat of a rebellion in south-west Ireland. Some went to Spain and joined the famous Spanish navy fleet. Others went to Holland and ended up fighting the Spanish. When the lord protector of England, Oliver Cromwell, invaded Ireland in the 1650s, around 30,000 men left. Some of them joined Irish brigades in Spain and France.

A tragic scene

After the Treaty of Limerick in 1691, around 16,000 rebels went to France. These men became known as the Wild Geese. In the Treaty of Limerick, the wives and children of the rebels had been promised places on the ships with their husbands. When the men were on board there was no room for all the families, so thousands of women and children were left behind in Ireland to beg for money and food – or to starve. Many women and children drowned trying to cling on to the boats as they set sail.

▶ *This 'Treaty Stone' in Limerick commemorates the Treaty of Limerick, signed in 1691. By the terms of the Treaty, the rebels were given free transport to Europe.*

Ferocious fighters

Irish troops in Europe soon earned a reputation for being fierce fighters, and they learned many skills in the European armies. Their wives and children often went into battle with them, but if the men were killed, the women and children were forced to become beggars. Many girls married other Irish exiles and so small communities of Irish grew up in France, Spain and Holland.

Emigration into the armies of Europe continued into the eighteenth century – then America began to offer a better future for Irish exiles.

The Caribbean

Many rebellions took place during the centuries that Ireland was ruled by England. Ordinary people in Ireland were very poor, and in some places the English government took away their tiny farms and brought in settlers from Scotland to cultivate the land instead. Faced with thousands of hungry, angry Irish men and women, the government chose to send some of them away to other countries that England ruled.

Transportation

While England was fighting the people of Ireland, it was also seizing islands in the Caribbean and creating sugar and tobacco plantations there. Local people were forced to work on the plantations and slaves were brought in from Africa. Starting under the rule of Oliver Cromwell in the mid-seventeenth century, Irish people were persuaded or forced to go out to the Caribbean. Between 1652 and 1658 – the period when Cromwell ruled England and Ireland – 50,000 Irish men, women and children were sent to Barbados and other islands in the West Indies that England controlled.

▲ Oliver Cromwell attacks the Irish after his invasion in 1649. This led to many Irish people fleeing to places like the Caribbean to escape English rule.

Others found their own way to the Caribbean. Many Irish people who had been sent as prisoners to America left there when they had served their prison sentences and went to islands such as St Kitt's, Barbados, Jamaica and Montserrat.

Montserrat

Montserrat is a tiny island that has been ruled by the English since the seventeenth century. Large numbers of Irish people found a home there. By 1650, there were about 2,000 Irish living on the island and only 1,000 English. Over the next few decades more Irish people joined the settlement. As they grew richer they bought land and eventually became part of the island's rich ruling class, owning slaves and growing sugar and coffee.

The St Patrick's Day Rebellion

On St Patrick's Day in 1768, a group of black slaves on Montserrat planned to attack the home of the island's governor. Many of the rich, white planters who would be at his St Patrick's Day party were Irish. They would be unarmed, and the slaves planned to kill as many as they could and then escape. The slaves were betrayed and the attack was prevented. Six were executed and 30 imprisoned. Create the front page of a newspaper, giving your own account of the attack, its failure and the punishment of the slaves. Use a strong headline and draw a picture to accompany your article.

It is a long time since the original Irish settlers married local people on Montserrat, but Irish place names such as Kinsale, and family names such as Lynch, Ryan and Farrell, have survived there. It is the only country outside Ireland that celebrates a national holiday on St Patrick's Day (17 March).

▲ Many Caribbean islands still have evidence of Irish settlers. This sign on O'Reilly Street in Cuba reads: 'Two island peoples in the same sea of struggle and hope: Cuba and Ireland.'

Canada

The Irish were among the first English-speaking people to settle in Canada, and it was never used as a prison for Irish convicts. Irish people were emigrating to Canada in the 1600s and by 1850 as many as 100,000 were travelling there from Ireland every year.

Early settlers

Canada was a welcoming place for Irish settlers. With a little cash or a government loan Irish emigrants could buy land for five shillings an acre. They had to cut down the forest, build their own homes and prepare the land for crops and animals. Poorer people could find work as lumberjacks, or as dock workers or farm labourers. They might even be able to save enough money to buy their own place. Many Irish people became wealthy and powerful. Some of their children became lawyers, doctors and politicians.

As early as 1763 a man from County Tyrone in Ireland, Guy Carleton, became governor of Quebec and was later governor-general of Canada for 10 years. Another Irishman, Colonel Talbot de Malahide, established 29 towns with Irish settlers in Ontario.

Irishman Guy Carleton served as governor of Quebec twice. The map below shows the main areas of Irish settlement in Canada.

Northwest Territories

Newfoundland

British Columbia

Ontario

Quebec

Grosse Ile

Coffin ships

Between 1845 and 1851 the Great Famine brought hard times for people in Ireland. Thousands of people left the country, heading for Canada in the hope of escaping starvation and disease. Many died during the journey from hunger or illnesses such as cholera or typhoid. The ships that carried them across the ocean were known as 'coffin ships' because so many people died in them. The Irish people were brought to secluded places on the coast of Canada, where the sick and dying were kept in very poor conditions until the epidemic was over.

Irish people contributed a great deal to the progress of their new country, and today about four million people in Canada can claim that their ancestors were Irish.

The Jeanie Johnston *was one of the 'coffin ships' that carried Irish emigrants to the New World. This replica ship can be visited in County Kerry in Ireland.*

What does a pioneer need?

Imagine you are an early pioneer settler in Canada. You have a piece of forest and a little money to get started. Discuss in groups of three or four what you would need to spend your money on. Look at the list below and choose the three most important items. How could you begin to make some money from your land? Can you think of any items not on the list that would be important?

- Horse
- Axe, saw, woodworking tools
- Gun and ammunition
- Wood
- Seeds
- Cow
- Furniture

Transportation to Australia

Irish people first went to Australia as convicts, sent there by the British government from Cork in 1791. Their crimes included stealing clothes or food, or rebelling against the government. The journey to Australia took 114 days and the convicts were kept in chains the whole time. Conditions on the boats were terrible, and many did not survive the journey.

After they had served their sentences in Australia, many convicts decided to stay there rather than return to Ireland. Their children became the first generation of Australian-Irish.

Invitations to Australia

From about 1830, the governors of Australian colonies began to invite Irish families to settle there. They offered cheap fares and sometimes grants of land.

Many of these settlers became successful farmers, using the skills that they had learned at home. Some became very wealthy landowners, others became wandering farm workers, who were known as 'swagmen'.

▶ *Swagmen would travel around the country, taking all their worldly possessions with them, earning money through temporary farming positions or odd jobs.*

Orphans

Between 1845 and 1851, when the Great Famine swept through Ireland, many young orphan girls were sent to Australia as possible wives for the settlers. Other settlers came out to join their families or brought their wives and children with them, but these young girls had no friends or relatives to help them. A few of them found work as maids and eventually got married, but many did not survive the harsh conditions of Australia.

The Australian Diaspora today

The population of Australia today is about 19 million. About one-third of Australians have Irish ancestors, making this the most Irish country in the world apart from Ireland itself. Most of these people come from Irish Catholic backgrounds, but there are also many people descended from Ulster Protestant families.

Ned Kelly

Ned Kelly was born in 1854 to Irish parents. He and his brothers were outlaws and robbed trains and banks. Ned made himself a suit of armour, which he wore when he fought the police. Local people liked him and hid him from the police, but he was finally captured and hanged in 1880 at the age of 25. Use the web pages listed below to find out more about Ned Kelly's Irish background. Draw a family tree showing his brothers, parents and grandparents, and indicate where they were born. Use pictures from the Internet to illustrate the family tree.

- http://www.nedkellysworld.com.au/history/familytree/familytree.htm

- http://www.fethard.com/people/redkelly.html

- http://scs.une.edu.au/Bushrangers/kellys.htm

This picture from the Illustrated London News *of 11 September 1880 shows outlaw Ned Kelly just before he is captured by police. He is wearing a special suit of armour that he made himself.*

America: Before the Famine

The first Irish people to arrive in America were sent there by Oliver Cromwell in the seventeenth century. They were convicts, priests or vagrants. Their sentences ranged from seven years to life, during which time they worked on plantations. Those with shorter sentences were able to learn a trade and start a new life in America when they had served their time. After America gained independence from Britain in 1776, this transportation of convicts stopped.

▶ *Five of the signatories of the American Declaration of Independence, plus the man who printed it, were Ulster Irish who fought against Britain in the American War of Independence.*

The first emigrants

In 1704 the British parliament passed a law making every British subject – including Irish people – take an oath of allegiance to the Church of England. In Ireland most people were Roman Catholics. Rather than take this oath of allegiance many of them chose to emigrate to America, where they hoped they would be able to follow their own beliefs. At this time there were very few white people in America and the British government encouraged people to go there to start farms or to work in the new factories and businesses in the towns.

The first settlers were from Ulster – the nine counties in the north of Ireland. Many of them were skilled workers and had a little money. They went to Philadelphia and travelled south. There they could claim a piece of land and farm it for free.

An Irish settler wrote to the *Times* newspaper in London, explaining how pleased he was with his new life:

> '*I am exceedingly well pleased at coming to this land of plenty. On arrival I purchased 120 acres of land at $5 an acre. You must bear in mind that I have purchased the land out, and it is to me and mine an "estate for ever", without a landlord, an agent or tax-gatherer to trouble me. I would advise all my friends to quit Ireland – the country most dear to me; as long as they remain in it they will be in bondage and misery.*'

Those who had no money to pay their fare to America would make a deal with the ship owner. They would work for him for five years. The ship owner could sell their labour to farmers or factory owners during that time if he did not need their labour himself. These emigrants were often treated very badly. Farmers looked after their slaves because they were valuable and belonged to the farmer outright. Slaves would work for the farmer all their lives. The Irish labourers were only of value to a farmer for five years.

Joseph Murphy

At the age of 12 Joseph Murphy emigrated to America with his parents. In 1839 he started a wagon-making business in St Louis. Most horse-drawn wagons of the time could carry about 453 kilograms. Joseph invented a new wagon that could carry 2,265 kilograms. These became the covered wagons that the thousands of settlers travelling west used to carry their belongings in the wagon trains.

▲ Covered wagons were important to the early emigrants in America. They allowed them to travel the long distances to their settlements with all their possessions. These emigrants are in the Loup Valley in Nebraska.

America: After the Famine

By 1840, Irish people were spreading throughout the newly independent country of America. Two different groups of Irish people lived in the cities: Catholics and Protestants. There were far more Protestant Irish than Catholic at this time. These two groups did not mix with each other, but occasionally there were fights between them.

Famine strikes

In Ireland, the millions of poor people who lived in the countryside depended on potatoes to survive. In 1845 the potato harvest was destroyed by a disease called blight.

The same thing happened the following year. Whole families died of starvation and those who travelled to the cities for help caught diseases such as typhoid or cholera and died. Thousands decided to emigrate to America in order to stay alive. They travelled on cargo ships that had brought timber to Ireland and were returning to North America. Conditions were terrible and thousands of people died at sea or in quarantine in Canada or America.

▶ *This is a scene at Cork harbour in Ireland in 1851. The boards are advertising passages to places like Boston in America and Quebec in Canada.*

After the Famine

So many people were fleeing to America that several places on the eastern seaboard, including New York, passed laws regulating who could enter the country. Passengers had to prove that they had enough money to survive, and each ship was restricted in the number of passengers it could bring into America.

The largest numbers of Irish arrived in New York. There they found work as labourers building roads and canals. Those in the worst condition lived in slums and begged on the streets in order to survive. Many died.

Between 1847 and 1851, 850,000 Irish people arrived in New York alone. Those who found jobs saved money to send home so that their relatives could eventually afford to join them in America.

Irish Americans today

Irish people settled in America and their children prospered. Today, people with ancestors from Ireland number 43 million. Many past American presidents have Irish ancestors and people of Irish descent proudly celebrate this on St Patrick's Day.

◀ *US president Andrew Jackson's parents both came from Country Antrim in Ireland.*

The Irish Emigrant Society

In 1847 the Irish Emigrant Society was formed in New York to help the thousands of Irish people who were arriving in the city. What kind of help do you think they most needed? List the ways in which the society could have helped.

◀ *An Irish immigrant family arriving in New York in 1926. This woman's husband has already gone to America and she is joining him, with 10 of their 21 children.*

New Zealand

In 1796 New Zealand was a small trading post with just a few Europeans living fairly peacefully alongside the Maori, the native inhabitants of the island. As more Europeans arrived, wars broke out between white settlers and the Maori. Irish soldiers in the British army fought against the Maori until 1872, when the British finally gained control of New Zealand.

▲ Maoris perform a war dance in front of British army officers in New Zealand.

The Gold Rush

In the 1860s gold was discovered in the west and south of New Zealand and about 25,000 Irish men from Australia and Britain came to the islands to look for new gold fields and to work in the mines. Trouble often broke out between Irish people of Catholic and Protestant descent, just as it did in America.

▶ This map of New Zealand shows where the Gold Rush (orange dots) was focused, which drew so many Irish there. It also shows the locations of Irish settlement across both islands (black dots).

Auckland

Thames

Taranaki

Wellington

Hokitika

Christchurch

Otago

Port Chalmers

Assisted passage

The largest waves of Irish emigration to New Zealand began in the 1870s, when the government of New Zealand began to recruit new emigrants from Ireland – both women and men. The men were needed to work on the many government building projects that were underway in New Zealand, and the women took jobs as maids in the houses of the wealthier white settlers. Between 1870 and 1914 about 2,000 emigrants from Ireland arrived in New Zealand each year.

The emigrants were mostly poor, unskilled workers, like those who went to Australia. Unlike the earliest Australian emigrants, however, who were sent there as convicts, these emigrants arrived by choice. Like the Australian and American Irish they saved money so they could afford to bring their families over. Some of them found work on farms using the skills they had learned in Ireland.

Most Irish people prospered in New Zealand. They experienced less discrimination than the Irish in America or Australia. By 1900, the Irish made up about one-fifth of the white population of New Zealand.

New Zealand today

New Zealanders of Irish descent remember their heritage in various ways. There are Orange Day parades on 12 July to celebrate a famous battle in Ireland when Protestant forces defeated the Catholic King James II in 1690. St Patrick's Day is also celebrated with parades and parties. A few Irish people married local Maoris, and the chief of the Ngai Tahu tribe on South Island, of mixed Irish and Maori descent, is Sir Tipene O'Regan. Many people of Irish descent are business and political leaders.

Compare New Zealand and Ireland

Irish people did particularly well in New Zealand. Find out more about the country – its weather and geography. What similarities are there between New Zealand and Ireland? Why do you think the Irish did well there? What difference do you think it makes that New Zealand was never a penal colony?

South America

The first Irish people to set foot on South American soil are thought to have been two cabin boys who sailed with the explorer Ferdinand Magellan in the sixteenth century. Later that century, the first European colonists – including Irish – founded Buenos Aires.

Irish saviours

More Irish arrived in South America with the many missionaries who travelled there. There were also Irishmen among the soldiers in the conquering European armies. As the soldiers settled in South America, they often changed sides, joining the local people in their wars against the conquerors.

In the eighteenth century Ambrosio O'Higgins from Sligo became the viceroy of Peru and protected farmers from Spanish settlers who wanted to take their land. His son, Bernardo, joined the armies of Chile and fought to liberate the country from its conquerors.

The Irish in Argentina

Argentina attracted many Irish people. In the eighteenth century Irish settlers realised that there was plenty of land there that could be used. There were also thousands of wild cattle and sheep that could be caught and farmed, to make a good living. These settlers recruited Irish tanners and butchers, created huge estates and became very wealthy. By 1880 about 40,000 Irish people had settled in Argentina and owned 20 million sheep. Irish estate owners encouraged the development of railways to transport their meat, leather and wool. They introduced steam-powered machinery and bred high-quality animals. All this was done, though, at the cost of the native people, who were driven off their land or killed.

Argentine revolutionary Che Guevara could trace his lineage back to Galway, in the west of Ireland, through his father's line.

The Kavanagh Building is the tallest in Argentina. It was commissioned by Corina Kavanagh, a wealthy woman of Irish descent.

Camila O'Gorman and Uladislao Gutierrez

Camila O'Gorman's father and brothers were all leading figures in Argentina in the early nineteenth century, and she might have married well and lived a life of luxury. However, she fell in love with a priest, Uladislao Gutierrez, and they ran away together. They were eventually discovered by a relative, taken to Buenos Aires and, with the approval of Camila's Irish father, executed by firing squad. Why do you think they would be treated so harshly? Write a letter from Camila to her father from her prison cell explaining why she ran away. What else might she want to say to him? Use the website below to help you.

■ http://www.irlandeses.org/julianello.htm

Today about 300,000 Irish Argentineans live in Argentina, speaking English and preserving their Irish traditions. Some of the wealthiest people in the country have Irish roots.

Leaving for Britain

For 800 years Irish people have been emigrating to Britain in search of a better life, away from the rebellions and poverty in Ireland. By the eighteenth century, the fare for a journey to Britain by ship was less than a day's wages.

In the nineteenth century Britain was one of the wealthiest countries in the world, and Ireland was one of Europe's poorest. Irish people travelled to towns in Britain to take up work in factories and mills, or building roads and canals.

Irish communities in England

Small communities of Irish people developed on the outskirts of cities such as Liverpool, Manchester and London. Many Irish people took up summer work on farms, tending and harvesting crops. Each year after the harvest they returned to Ireland. Some weavers from the linen industry in Ulster emigrated to the weaving towns of Lancashire, where the pay was better than in Ireland. Others travelled to Britain for a short time to make some money before moving on to Australia or America. Many Irish people joined the ranks of the British army or found government jobs in British colonies such as India.

Between 1847 and 1857 as many as two million people emigrated from Ireland. Many of them arrived in ships in the docks at Liverpool.

◀ *Industry flourished in Britain in the nineteenth century. Irish workers were used on construction projects like this – laying the foundations for a row of engineering workshops at the Thames Dockyard in 1865.*

Accurate records were never kept of how many settled in Britain, but newspaper accounts describe the terrible state they were in:

'Ireland is pouring into the cities, and even into the villages of this island, a fetid *mass of famine, nakedness and dirt and fever. Liverpool ... seems destined to become one mass of disease.'*

The Times, *2 April 1847*

Those who survived experienced hatred and fear in Britain because people thought that they might catch diseases from them. The Irish emigrants often had to be given food and money by local governments and people resented that, too. They were also feared and despised because most of them were Catholic, and Britain was very anti-Catholic at the time.

Emigrant choices

From 1800 to 1914 Britain was the second favourite place for Irish emigrants to go to. The first choice was America. Why do you think that these Irish people would choose to live in Britain rather than Australia, New Zealand or America?

▲ This is an anti-Irish cartoon from the satirical magazine Punch in 1846. The British were very wary of all the Irish workers who had arrived in the country.

The Irish in Britain

By 1900 about half a million people living in Britain were born in Ireland. Many more were second- or third-generation Irish. While the first emigrants were usually poor manual workers, their children often got better jobs.

The Second World War

When the Second World War began in 1939, thousands of British men had to join the army. Many Irish people took up the jobs that the men had left vacant in Britain. Even when the soldiers returned there were still plenty of jobs for the Irish. They slowly formed their own Irish communities in the cities. These areas often became Irish in character, and the people formed Irish social clubs and ran traditional Irish dance and music classes.

After the war

Think about what Britain must have been like at the end of the Second World War. Why would Irish people still be needed even though British soldiers had come home from the war? What kind of jobs might they take up? Write your answers as a list.

The late-twentieth century

In the 1970s Irish people were the largest immigrant group in Britain. Britain became involved in fighting in Northern Ireland. Many Catholic people there wanted to be part of Ireland, not Britain. A minority of extreme Republicans set off bombs and began fighting those who wanted to stay part of Britain. They set off bombs in England, too, and life became difficult for ordinary Irish people living there.

Since the Good Friday Agreement was reached in 1998, Northern Ireland is more peaceful, and so is life for Irish people in Britain.

▼ *Damage in London in 1973, after an Irish Republican Army (IRA) bomb went off.*

Irish footballers in England

Many talented Irish soccer players have become famous by joining English teams. One team in particular – Manchester United – has had many Irish players. Jackie Blanchflower and Harry Gregg, both Irish players, were part of the team that was involved in a plane crash in 1958, while in the 1950s two of the team's captains, Johnny Carey and Noel Cantwell, were Irish.

The long list of Irish men who have played for Manchester United includes George Best. Best was born in Belfast and scored 179 goals for Manchester in the 1960s and 1970s. Roy Keane is also one of the most famous names in recent soccer history. Born in Cork, he played for United for 12 years and then became manager of Sunderland. Most recently, John O'Shea from Waterford has started to make his name with Manchester United.

Former Manchester United player Roy Keane was born in County Cork in Ireland. As well as United, he played for his country and now manages English club Sunderland.

The Celtic Tiger

Today, Irish cities – especially Dublin – attract settlers from all over the world. Now more people are arriving in Ireland than are leaving it.

From the seventeenth century until the mid-1990s, Ireland was a poor country, often at war with its British rulers. The only choice for millions of Irish people who wanted a better life was emigration. But in the 1990s Ireland gradually became a wealthy country with lots of jobs for all its young people. This wave of prosperity began to be known as the Celtic Tiger.

People who leave Ireland now do so because they want to experience life in other countries. They are skilled, professional people. They take up well-paid work all over the world, which they often do for a few years before returning home.

A new Ireland

In all the centuries of emigration, very few people from abroad ever went to live in Ireland. It was rare to see black or Asian or South American people in Ireland anywhere other than Dublin.

Recently an enormous change has taken place, as people from all over the world have settled there. They mostly take up low-paid work, just as the Irish emigrants once did. Immigrants have added to the quality of life in Ireland, introducing their music, food and festivals. Sometimes they have encountered hatred and prejudice, just as the Irish did when they were immigrants.

The Diaspora today

All over the world, but especially in Australia and New Zealand, America and Britain, the Irish Diaspora has had an enormous impact.

Many countries can name Irish people who have changed their country's history for the better. Third- and fourth-generation Irish people remember their Irish roots and in various ways still practise the customs of their Irish ancestors – in Irish dance, music and religion. Irish people as far away as America and Australia follow Irish politics and listen to Irish music. Their children might learn the tin whistle, the bodhrán or uilleann pipes, or learn Irish dancing. They celebrate their Irishness on 17 March, St Patrick's Day, with parades and parties. Most of all they keep their connections with those who stayed behind, returning to their ancestors' homes to see where it all started.

Making friends

In the last decade or so some elderly people in rural areas of Ireland have met people with a different colour skin for the first time. Write a short conversation between a new immigrant to Ireland and an elderly farmer in the Irish countryside. What might they talk about? Their different backgrounds? What life is like in each of their native countries? What they might have in common? Act out this dialogue with a friend.

▲ All over the world, people celebrate their Irish heritage. This Irish pub is in the Dominican Republic in the Caribbean.

Glossary

ancestors — the people in someone's family who lived in earlier times, e.g. grandparents, great grandparents.

betrayed — given away to the enemy.

bodhrán — a drum made from a goatskin stretched over a wooden frame.

Catholic — someone who follows a form of Christianity that believes in the authority of the pope and the Bible.

cholera — a serious disease caused by infected water or food.

colonies — areas of land settled and ruled by people from another country.

convicts — people who have been found guilty of a crime and have been given a prison sentence.

descendants — the people in someone's family who come after them, such as their children, grandchildren and great grandchildren.

discrimination — when someone is treated badly because of their race, sex or religion.

emigration — when someone leaves their country of birth to go and live abroad.

epidemic — when a disease affects large numbers of people in the same area all at once, spreading from person to person.

exiles — people who are forced to leave their own country and live somewhere else.

fetid — unhealthy and polluted.

generation — all the people in a family or community who are born around the same time.

Good Friday Agreement — agreement reached in 1998 between the government of Britain, the Republican groups who wanted Northern Ireland to join the Republic of Ireland and the Unionist groups who wanted to stay part of Britain, in which they agreed to stop fighting and find a way to live peacefully.

Great Famine — the name of the famine that swept through Ireland from 1845, caused by the failure of the potato crop. Thousands of people died of starvation or emigrated to escape.

immigrant — someone who has just arrived in a country and intends to live there.

liberate — to set a person or a country free.

lumberjacks — people whose job it is to cut down trees for wood.

manual workers — people who do physical jobs requiring no special level of education or training – often poorly paid.

mercenaries — people who fight as part of an army for payment rather than loyalty to that particular country.

missionaries — people who go to another country in order to convert its population to their religion.

Northern Ireland	six counties in the north of Ireland which remained part of Britain after the rest of Ireland became independent in 1921.
oath of allegiance	a solemn promise to be loyal to a country or to a leader.
Oliver Cromwell	ruler of England between 1649 and 1658. He invaded Ireland and is remembered there for the murder of thousands of people.
penal colony	a settlement in another country that operates as a prison for criminals from the ruling country.
pioneer	someone who travels to a place where no one has lived before and makes a home for themselves using the materials around them.
Protestant	someone who follows a form of Christianity that rejects the teachings of the Roman Catholic Church and believes in the Bible as the only authority for Christians.
quarantine	a place apart from other people where those who have caught a contagious disease can be looked after until they are well.
rebellion	a fight against the government.
recruit	to pay or encourage someone to join you, or a person who has been persuaded to join.
Republicans	people living in Ireland who want all the counties of Ireland to be part of the Republic of Ireland.
secluded	lonely or isolated.
sentence	the punishment decided on by a judge after someone is found guilty of a crime – usually a term in prison, or a fine or, in some countries, execution.
subject (British)	anyone born in Britain or any of its colonies.
tanners	people whose job it is to prepare animal skins to make into leather.
transportation	sending people to one of the prison colonies as a punishment.
Treaty of Limerick	an agreement signed in 1691 between Irish rebels and the government of England led by William of Orange. The rebels were given free transport to Europe.
typhoid	a serious infection caused by contaminated water or food.
Ulster	Nine counties in the north of Ireland: Antrim, Armagh, Cavan, Derry, Donegal, Down, Fermanagh, Monaghan and Tyrone.
uilleann pipes	a set of musical pipes played by forcing air from a leather bag through the pipes.
vagrants	people who have no home or job.
viceroy	the ruler of a colony.

For teachers and parents

The Irish Diaspora is a complex and emotive subject, and many myths have arisen about it. These relate to the proportions of Catholics to Protestants in the various countries, the attitudes of those who emigrated, the sense of the Diaspora as referring to victims rather than courageous and sometimes aggressive people, the behaviour of emigrants towards other minority groups and towards each other. For every emigrant diary or first-hand account of an emigration there is a fallible person writing the words. Children should be encouraged to recognise that they are dealing with opinions as much as fact, and should evaluate the evidence with care.

SUGGESTED FURTHER ACTIVITIES

Pages 4–5 What is the Diaspora?

The Irish are not the only ethnic group to have formed a diaspora. Many other races have fled to foreign countries as refugees or economic migrants. Children could research other ethnic groups that have chosen or been forced to leave their homelands and find out the reasons: Palestinians, West Indians, Rwandans, Asians, Chinese, Jews, Albanians etc. Children from different ethnic backgrounds might be able to add their own family's history.

Pages 6–7 The Wild Geese

The expression 'Wild Geese' has been applied to many groups of people who fled Ireland over the years of British rule. Children could consider why they would be called this. What is it about wild geese that evokes the sadness of these flights?

Students could look at http://indigo.ie/~wildgees/wildgees.htm, the website of the Wild Geese Heritage Museum, and find out just how many exoduses there were, when they happened and why. *The Encyclopaedia of Ireland* also has a good account.

Pages 8–9 The Caribbean

Encyclopaedia Britannica has an account of the uprising of the slaves in Montserrat. Accounts of who betrayed the slaves vary. Begin a discussion with pupils about slavery and the similarities and differences between indentured servants and slaves. Mention that slave owners took better care of their slaves than their indentured Irish servants because they only had the Irish for the five years of their sentence, while they had the black slaves as long as they lived.

Children could discuss why people who had been treated so badly by their English masters would treat black people in the same way or worse.

Pages 10–11 Canada

An Irish family living in Ontario in the nineteenth century called Donnelly became as infamous as Ned Kelly. Children could look up the family at www.mysteriesofcanada.com and make a children's book about their lives, illustrating it with pictures of their exploits.

One ship, the *Jeanie Johnston*, carried passengers in a humane way and only a small proportion of its passengers died. A replica of the ship has been built and http://www.jeaniejohnston.net/history.html gives an illustrated account of the original ship and the conditions on board. Children could visit the website and draw a typical emigrant's living space in the ship.

Pages 12–13 Transportation to Australia

Children could investigate which crimes were punished by transportation and look up the history and establishment of penal colonies in Australia. Where were they set up and why? What was life like in a penal colony?

They could find out why people chose to stay in Australia rather than returning to Ireland. What factors might have influenced this decision?

Pages 14–15 America: Before the Famine

Children could find the list of signatories of the American Declaration of Independence and find out which ones were of Irish descent.

In America the expressions 'Ulster Scots' and 'Irish Americans' denotes people of Ulster Protestant and Irish Catholic descent. Students could discuss why the two groups of people might want to distinguish themselves in that way. This could lead to a discussion of the meaning of nationality. What makes someone Irish, English etc.?

For successful emigrants America must have seemed wonderful. Students could write a letter home, telling their families what life was like.

Pages 16–17 America: After the Famine

Children could research the background of some of the more infamous Irish Americans:
• Billy the Kid: www.aboutbillythekid.com
• Sam Brannan: www.pbs.org/weta/thewest/people/a_c/brannan.htm
• Davy Crockett: www.folkpark.com/children'scorner/emigrationstories/
• Typhoid Mary Mallon: http://history1900s.about.com/od/1900s/a/typhoidmary.htm

They could investigate the history of the Native Americans and the impact of European settlers on their way of life. This could lead to a discussion of the ways in which the two groups could have found a peaceful settlement.

Pages 18–19 New Zealand

Lots of people saved up cash to bring out their relatives. Children could write a letter home telling their relatives what to expect and suggesting what useful things they could bring out on their journey. What things might not be readily available in New Zealand which could be bought in Dublin?

Research the contrasting lives between Maoris and settlers. How would the two cultures clash?

Drama work: divide the class into two groups – settlers and Maoris. Have them act out a drama in which they discuss the problems and the issues that exist between them.

Children could research some famous New Zealanders and trace their Irish links:
• All Blacks
• Martin Cash, gentleman bush ranger
• Christopher Reilly, William Fox, who discovered the gold fields
• William Hobson, New Zealand's first governor from Waterford
• Jim Bolger, who was prime minister until the 1990s

Pages 20–21 South America

Children could find and copy a map of South America and mark on it the places in the text and other locations where they know Irish people settled.

Each student could choose one South American country and find out about famous Irish people from that country. They could make a presentation about that country and how the Irish settlers managed.

Pages 22–23: Leaving for Britain

Children could look at a map of Britain and decide which towns the Irish emigrants might arrive at first, considering that the only means of transport was a boat. Why would there be more Irish in the west of Britain than in the east? What were the main ports and cities where the Irish settled?

Pages 24–25 The Irish in Britain

Many Irish people who emigrated to Britain during the Second World War returned to Ireland when they retired. Which country do you think would be most familiar to them after perhaps 40 years of living in Britain? Why would British Irish be more likely to retire to Ireland than, for example, Australian or American Irish?

Children with Irish connections could ask their relatives (particularly grandparents) what life was like after the war in Ireland or Britain. Ireland in the 1950s and 1960s still had areas with no electricity or running water, phones or domestic appliances. They could then write a conversation between English/American and Irish cousins about the differences in their lives. Children with no Irish connections could try to find a neighbour, preferably Irish but not necessarily so, whose parents/grandparents moved to Britain from another country.

Pages 26–27 The Celtic Tiger

Children could mark on a map of the world all the places that Irish people settled. Another map could show the places where immigrants to Ireland have come from.

Children could find out what the expression Celtic Tiger means. Why would this affect emigration and immigration?

In the years before aeroplanes or steamships the journey was long and dangerous. Children could find out how long it would take to reach each of the destinations by sail.

Which time period would have been the best one to be emigrating in?
• The Great Famine
• Cromwell's transportations
• Transportation to Australia
• Assisted passage to New Zealand
• Britain during the Second World War

BOOKS AND WEBSITES

Brian Lalor, ed., *The Encyclopaedia of Ireland* (Gill & Macmillan, 2003) An excellent brief account of the countries Irish people settled in, the Diaspora, transportation and related matters.

Tim Pat Coogan, *Wherever Green is Worn* (Hutchinson, 2000) Contains fascinating anecdotes of individual Irish lives.

Thomas Keneally, *The Great Shame* (Chatto & Windus, 1998) Contains an account of the Irish in Australia.

Marita Conlon McKenna, *Under the Hawthorn Tree* (O'Brien Press, 2002) A fictional account of children during the Irish Famine.

www.irelandroots.com has information on the numbers of people estimated to have emigrated to each country plus links to Irish association websites for each country and articles on individual Irish emigrants.

www.allaboutirish.com includes some original emigrants' accounts of their journeys from the nineteenth century.

http://journals.aol.co.uk/iis04/SHP has lots of schools' materials on the Famine and emigration.

www.aoh61.com/history/mainhist.htm has some excellent links to accounts of the Irish in baseball, the Molly Maguires, the history of the Diaspora and accounts of the Irish in some of the lesser known destinations for emigrants.

www.irish-society.org/archives.htm has links to pages on Grosse Ile, the Famine, the Irish in America, Montserrat, Irish soldiers in Mexico.

www.folkpark.com/childrens-corner/emigrationstories has stories of various famous emigrants.

Index